PROFIT WITH YOUR PERSONALITY

PROFIT WITH YOUR PERSONALITY

───◦◦∿∿◦◦───

LEARN HOW TOP PRODUCERS WIN
AT LEAD GENERATION, AND HOW
YOU CAN TOO

DR. LEE DAVENPORT

CONTENTS

Tying it All Together

THE NOD

What Others Are Saying

*If you want to learn from the best of the best, read Dr. Lee Davenport's new book, **Profit with Your Personality**. As a real estate coach and trainer, Dr. Lee has written a thoughtful and insightful guide for REAL-TORS® and Brokers to provide them with actionable tips to bring their business to the 'next level.' Rather than a 'one size fits all approach' Dr. Lee focuses on how REAL-TORS® can tap into their personal strengths to become Top Producers. This easy-to-read guide is a must-have for those who are looking to succeed.*

—**Sandy Krueger,** CEO, Staten Island Board of REALTORS®

Dr. Lee Davenport has led the real estate industry to embrace technology and social media. Her thought leadership in this area has impacted agents and brokers across the country. But more than just her track record, my admiration of Dr. Lee stems from her warmth and compassion towards each individual she interacts with. Rare that you find such a beautiful combination and I am proud to call her a friend.

—**Stefanie Diaz,** Named one of Atlanta's Startup Wonder Women as the Founder of Mastermind Your Launch and a Popular Radio Host

———

True success is born out of an acute self-awareness, strong work ethic, and abiding determination. In this book, Dr. Lee will walk you through a process of self-evaluation to pinpoint what is and is not working in your business plan, and she will give you the courage to try new tactics until you find that perfect fit.

—**Erica Christoffer,** REALTOR® Magazine's Broker to Broker Consultant

EDITOR'S FOREWORD

Erica Christoffer, REALTOR®
Magazine's Broker to Broker Consultant

Dr. Lee Davenport won't let preconceived notions about introverts or extroverts stand in anyone's way to success in the field of real estate.

For more than two years, I've been editing articles and blog posts written by Lee for REALTOR® Magazine. As a real estate coach and trainer, she continually offers sound business advice for those new to the industry, as well as for veteran brokerage owners and managers looking to expand the tools in their arsenal. What I've found is that she consistently offers actionable tips that a reader can implement immediately. This book is no different.

Too often, people assume that there's a singular magic formula for making it in this business, and that formula is typically built around the extroverted personality type. But the fact of the matter is, there is a multitude of magic formulas as broad and diverse as the real estate markets across the U.S. Personalities, generally, fall on a spectrum with introverted and extroverted on the extreme ends. Lee will help you tailor your business to what comes most natural to you as an individual, no matter where you fall on that spectrum.

True success is born out of an acute self-awareness, strong work ethic, and abiding determination. In this book, Lee will walk you through a process of self-evaluation to pinpoint what is and is not working in your business plan, and she will give you the courage to try new tactics until you find that perfect fit.

THE SALESPERSON'S STRUGGLE

Introduction

You love houses. Or, maybe you love the generational wealth potential of real estate as an investment vehicle. Perhaps you love the thrill of connecting with new people and helping them navigate one of their most expensive transactions successfully.

Now, however, whatever got you involved in residential real estate sales may be a distant memory if you are struggling to generate leads (a.k.a. new business contacts and prospects). "Why?" you wonder. *Why am I not successful yet? Why did I think I could do this? Why am I not a top producer? Why did the "fail-proof" method of "Sally Sales-A-Lot" NOT work for me?* You are plagued with wondering **why**. You may even feel hopeless and have started your search online for job positions that will allow you to return to your former work life or help you start a second, third or fourth career.

Pause.

What if you *can* generate leads, necessary to have a thriving residential real estate sales business but, you just do not know how to do so yet? The key question to ask here is not simply **why** but rather **how**. *How can I succeed in this career? How can I become a top producer? How can I hit my business goals?*

> "THE ANSWERS ARE ALL OUT THERE, WE JUST NEED TO ASK THE RIGHT QUESTIONS."
>
> — Oscar Wilde

> "SUCCESSFUL PEOPLE ASK BETTER QUESTIONS, AND AS A RESULT, THEY GET BETTER ANSWERS."
>
> — Anthony Robbins

Asking **why** may leave us feeling inadequate as if we are not good enough for this career whereas wondering **how** often empowers us to proactively seek and execute a solution. Thus, before abandoning your sales dreams, I want to share with you a perspective that you may not have ever thought of or seriously considered. I want to share with you the **how** that I found among the nation's top producers that can change how you see lead generation.

———

YOUR CURRENT PERSPECTIVE

WHICH OF THE FOLLOWING STATEMENTS
ARE TRUE?

- Sales is a Numbers Game
- Sales Careers are Only for Extroverts

- There is Only One Formula for Sales Success
- Top Producers Figure Out What Lead Generation Activities Work Best for Them

As a real estate coach and former realty managing broker, I frequently hear our industry's myths and frustrations. But, I have also witnessed the best practices that unfortunately seem to be well-hidden secrets for some. Each true or false statement above represents an absolute truth for many of us, and for others, unquestionable falsehood.

YOUR TURN

I want to challenge you to throw out whatever you have heard, ESPECIALLY if you are not seeing the results you desire in your sales. Be open to what will unfold in the following pages that will give you new, inspiring insight on the true or false statements above, along with other industry customs and conventions that may not be rooted in today's reality.

Join me on a journey through the pages of this book to target a new sense of success within you. You can do more than you know... so prepare to transform what you know! Happy reading!

HERE'S THE ISSUE...

What are the issues holding you back? Your temptation may be to skip ahead to find the top producer best practices. If you do, you may miss making a discovery about yourself that is key to your long-term success. Get to the heart of the matter in this part. No one can be you like you so just say, "No" to skipping ahead!

YOU HUFF &
PUFF BUT
ZILCH

Chapter 1

The tale of the Three Little Pigs is a children's classic. You likely know this story. You may have even been afraid of the wolf as a child. But did you know this wolf can represent a modern-day salesperson? Now, that is not to say my fellow salespeople are ferocious wild animals hungry for livestock. Instead, often we are hungry for income and sales, and we let our hunger drive our interactions.

We historically have empathized with the pigs, but let us look closer at the wolf, starting with what the wolf did well. The wolf knew where his business leads lived. Just knowing where to go to find the leads is a big factor in the sales struggle for many of us, so kudos, Mr. Wolf.

Next, the wolf had a strategy to connect with those leads. The wolf went door-knocking as his lead generation method. He was not good at it! Like many salespeople today, before the wolf could get out his entire sales spiel, the pigs were running away from him.

They did not want what he was selling, and they were not going to stick around to hear his sales presentation.

He went toe-to-toe with the very pigs he was trying to win over. And, unfortunately, the wolf's frustration got the best of him, not uncommon for emotionally charged salespeople, who let the heat of the moment and rejection infuriate them. Consequently, the wolf created such a destructive ruckus that word about him spread to the next pig before his arrival.

When word travels about you, when you get free, unsolicited publicity, either it is because you are just that good or just that bad. The wolf was the latter.

When the wolf arrived at the third pig's house, he was determined to not take no for an answer. His persistence only frightened and annoyed the pigs instead of winning them over, which salespeople are often unconsciously guilty of doing. The wolf wasted hours at the final brick abode yet still ended up in hot water, literally, going down the chimney and landing in a pot of boiling water.

This wolf messed up. He made the frequent mistake of most salespeople. He (and we) marry a *method* instead of focusing on and requiring *results*. After the first house, the wolf did not have the results he wanted. It was time for him to self-assess, but instead, he continued on full-steam ahead and repeated the same thing at the second pig's house, with the same lackluster results. Surely, he would self-reflect, adjust and tweak after a second strike out. He did not. He just barreled along to the third prospect more desperate, forceful and "salesy" than ever before with the worst of the three results.

Door knocking was not his *thang*, but somewhere along the line he likely saw another wolf succeed with that lead generation method and he just did not want to give it up. Doing the same things but expecting different results can drive anyone insane, not just this wolf.

YOUR TURN

What are you doing in your business that is not getting you to the desired result?

Is it time for you to:

- Stop it?
- Be retrained?
- Outsource the activity?
- Or, try something altogether new?

Who can mentor or coach you to help you make the right decision? **Bonus:** If you do not have someone in your immediate sphere to help you, feel free to reach out to me for one **complimentary** coaching session at http://www.LearnWithLee.REALTOR.

DR. LEE DAVENPORT

"I WANT THE TOP-PRODUCER FORMULA"

Chapter 2

"Can you help me?" desperately pleaded a prospective coaching client.

"What's the problem?" I asked concerned.

"I want to grow my business. I want the top-producer formula."

That is what we think, do we not? That there is just one equation (e. g. $X + Y = Success$) that works the same for each person that will produce and re-produce success.

The New York caller continued, "I have tried cold-calling, but I just can't wrap my brain around doing this every day for the rest of my career. I don't like cold-calling, but that is what most of the agents at my office do. If that is the formula for me to succeed, then I will make myself do it." The caller resigned to being uncomfortable for the sake of copying someone else's success formula.

Here is the problem with that outlook:

Square pegs do not properly fit into round holes. What do I mean by that?

Remember back when you, your children, or your "grands" were in kindergarten. They had all types of toys to help stimulate their mind while keeping them from sticking a fork in an outlet or annoying the dog. One popular toy included shape-styled blocks that fit into same-shaped cutouts. It could be considered a basic puzzle game. Children new to this toy often would take the triangle shape and try to stuff it into the rectangle, grab the star piece and bang it into the square piece and the like.

The problem was that the right pieces were not being put with the right cutout. Instead, the mismatched shapes were placed in the wrong areas. Frustrated, the child either thinks, "This toy is broken, throw it out" or "Make it fit, bang on the piece until it is in the desired spot." Both approaches cause damage.

Now enter the parent, teacher, or babysitter. The child is now coached on what works with each shape to correctly solve the puzzle. *Pop.* With excitement and glee, the kindergartener giggles and claps as the square shape smoothly slides into the square cutout.

The game was not defective. Nor, did the pieces need to be forced into the space. There only needed to be an understanding of what worked best in each area.

Likewise, the game of real estate sales is not broken or defective. Nor, can we force every salesperson into one area. Not everyone will fit and damage will likely result. We simply need coaching and guidance to understand where we, as salespeople, best fit. Remember that saying, "All I really need to know I

learned in Kindergarten" by Robert Ful-
ghum? Well, this analogy is no exception.

YOUR TURN

- What in your career seems broken or
  does not fit?
- From who can you seek guidance and
  coaching to help you recalibrate?

ONE SIZE
NEVER FITS
ALL

Chapter 3

I detest seeing tags in t-shirts that say, "One size fits all" because that one size NEVER does. Whether the shirt hugs you like a baby's onesie or drapes over you like a potato sack or Snuggie® Blanket, it is just not a fit for everyone. Similarly, mislabeled t-shirts are like our careers in residential real estate sales – different strokes are needed for different folks.

Here is the shocker:

> THERE IS NO ONE DISC
> PERSONALITY TYPE THAT
> *CANNOT* SUCCEED IN
> RESIDENTIAL REAL ESTATE SALES.

Did that make your brain go tilt? If you are like me, you have probably heard that only particular types of personality will do well in sales, whether real estate or otherwise. For those of us who are more reserved, we have likely acquiesced to that notion because doing the cold lead generation tactics (using outbound activities like cold calling and door knocking) have made us feel like the round peg being stuffed and banged into a square hole by an impatient kindergartener. It is uncomfortable, to say the least!

GEEK SPEAK

Business practitioners, including real estate firm managers, frequently use the DISC personality assessment to size up its sales force due to its ease of use and four simple dimensions. DISC profiles simply categorize the spectrum of our behaviors based on four prominent measures:

- Dominant (outgoing and task-oriented),
- Influencer (outgoing and people-oriented),
- Steady (introverted and people-oriented), and

- Conscientious (introverted and task-oriented).

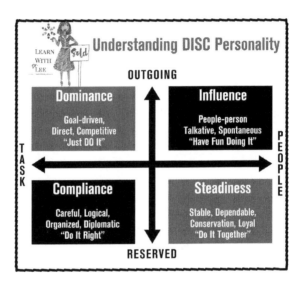

Among some companies, a prospective sales-person's predominant DISC personality type is relied upon to determine her overall aptness for a residential real estate sales career.

> WHAT WE SAY:
>
> The *RIGHT* Salesperson Personality
>
> =
>
> Sales Success

However, in my scholarly literature review of this topic, no significant correlation has been established between a salesperson's ultimate sales success and her preeminent DISC personality profile. Before you write a rebuttal, think about it this way: As managers, I have observed that we typically do not actually link a salesperson's personality profile to their ultimate sales success either. Rather, we associate a salesperson's personality with certain lead generation *methods,* particularly the methods we favor or the methods most used by our firm's sales team.

For example, we likely assess that someone who is reserved will have a hard time cold-calling (a method) while someone who is out-going and task-oriented, like the Dominant personality profile, will not. And, if we prefer our sales team to do cold-calling, we will more likely hire the Dominant person and dismiss the more introverted person. In essence, we have determined that the salesperson will not succeed with our customary lead generation methods. There is nothing wrong with that. But then we or the salesperson takes an unconnected leap, concluding the salesperson is completely unfit for real estate sales altogether. Unfortunately, a salesperson's success (or lack there of) with certain methods were confused with the salesperson's overall ability to succeed in sales.

We must separate lead generation methods from overall ability. Here is why.

Top Producer Best Practices

I recently conducted a university-based study that polled a portion of the top 1,000 residential real estate salespeople in the United States (U.S.). This study found:

> Top-producing residential real estate salespeople displayed "prominent personality types stemming from" *ALL* of the four DISC profiles; No one or two personality types were exclusive among the top sales professionals surveyed[1].

That means that "Chatty Cathy", typically seen as the Influencer personality style, is not the only type of top producer who can thrive in residential real estate sales. Real estate sales is not exclusive to the extroverted. This research proved that those of the more intro-verted natures (e.g. Steady and Conscien-tious) have achieved nationally recognized sales success too, which is no small feat in an

---

1. Davenport, L. D. (2017, March). Residential Real Estate Sales, Lead Generation and Personality: Trends from Top Producers (Doctoral dissertation, CalUniversity, 2017).

industry of more than 1 million profession-
als.

WHAT RESEARCH SUGGESTS:

Salesperson Personality

+

The *RIGHT* Lead-Gen. Activities

+

Consistency

=>

Success

This is ground-breaking research that should
help you breathe a sigh of relief. Why? The
results prove you do not have to take on
a fake persona in residential real estate sales
because this career field is not exclusive to
one or two personality types (as defined by
DISC). Your personality is not detestable in
sales. One size does not fit all. There are lead
generation methods that likely fit you
uniquely. In the next chapter, get ready to
find out what they are.

THE SECRET SAUCE

What are top producers doing to succeed? This is the section to highlight, underline, and post on your vision board so that you do not forget these vital sales pointers.

WHAT'S IN
YOUR HAND?

Chapter 4

Since we have been swapping best-loved narratives, one of my favorites is of David and his battle with the giant, Goliath. Like many of us, David learned about a new career opportunity that actually could change his family's financial situation. He was intrigued and gung-ho. He was ready to take this moment head on, despite the "hater-ade" and discouragement voiced by his brothers. We know that feeling — the excitement of a new and profitable possibility. Familial lack of confidence was no deterrent for David, and hopefully, you are pushing ahead with the same spirit of determination.

He was ready to take this moment head on, despite the "hater-ade" and discouragement voiced by his brothers. We know that feeling — the excitement of a new and profitable possibility. Familial lack of confidence was no deterrent for David. Hopefully, you are pushing ahead with the same spirit of determination.

David was clearing every hurdle of this race

until it was time to select his method of war-
fare. The King offered David his suit of
armor and sword. How exciting! Can you
imagine the top producer you have always
emulated saying to you, "Here is my lead generation system — I want you to have it"?
What a dream come true! I am sure David
was thrilled — he was going from an outsider
of the organization to using the top producer's personal best in a matter of hours.

Can you imagine the top producer you have
always emulated saying to you, "Here is my
lead generation system — I want you to have
it"? What a dream come true! I am sure
David was thrilled — he was going from an
outsider of the organization to using the top
producer's personal best in a matter of hours.

David tried on the armor and held the
sword. They fit him awkwardly. Regrettably,
he felt like the square peg being forced into a
round hole.

Unlike the wolf, David did not obsessively
stick with *a method* no matter how well it

worked for his predecessor. He paused to think about his *results* because he was not married to a **method.**

Top Producer Best Practices

David thought about his past victories, albeit in another profession, and used the common denominator of his success, which was the very things he had in his hand. For David, it was his slingshot and stone.

For you, it may be your way to disarm and connect with strangers. Or, you may be talented at crunching and relaying housing data and market analysis. You may be a social media influencer. You might have a way with the pen in sending thoughtful letters and emails. Perhaps, you are a rockstar at cold calling. The key is to know what is in your hand, what you have been gifted to do during your time on this earth.

YOUR TURN

- What is in your hand? What is the common denominator of your past successes that you still possess?

- How does this relate to your current sales situation?
- How can you implement more of what you uniquely do well?

SOME LIKE IT HOT

Chapter 5

Warm versus cold weather. Some people naturally flourish in one climate over the other. Case in point: I have a friend that is invigorated by the numbing cold of a northern, icy winter. He loves to don a fashionable scarf, a designer coat, and some name-brand boots. Oh, and I cannot overlook his wacky and wild sock game. He feels at his best when there is a chill in the air. There is a pep in his step, a smile on his face, and creativity in his work.

I, on the other hand, practically ran screaming from the north and its brutally cold winters for the warmer climate of "Hotlanta", where I love it. My pseudo-superpowers to get more done and think clearly seem to kick in as the days grow longer and warmer. Truthfully, I feel like I need to move even further south to get less of the cold season, go figure.

Some of us are comfortable in the cold while others of us are happy with a warm environment. It is okay to admit it and own it. And, so it goes in our lead generation life.

———

YOUR LEAD GENERATION CLIMATE

Some lead generation activities are cold in nature, meaning the person you are approaching does not know you, did not ask to know you, and surely did not ask for you, a stranger, to contact her. Consequently, you may get cursed at, hung up on, face a slammed door, or be reported as a spammer. Most people think of cold-calling as an example, which is spot-on. Just like cold weather warriors in parkas, those that are more suited for cold leads must have already clothed themselves in warmth, having a high self-esteem and high tolerance to cold rejection. "Thin skin" is not the right gear for cold lead generation methods.

Others may shine in warm environments of bright, smiling faces where you are approached and sought after instead of the other way around. This may be considered by some as the "if you build it, they will come" approach. Unbeknownst to some, there is a finesse to this technique that requires getting in front of and engaging with as many eyeballs as possible. Thus, it is really the "if you build it well, offer something of value (a.k.a. a lead magnet), and stay in front of a lot of people, they will come" approach. Examples include receiving calls from a well-crafted newsletter you sent out to past clients or connecting with people who found your swanky website and messaged you.

TOP PRODUCER BEST PRACTICES

Remarkably, a portion of the salespeople I surveyed from among the top producing

1,000 residential salespeople in the nation attested that:

> THEY ***NEVER*** APPROACH
> STRANGERS FOR NEW BUSINESS[1].

They take the warm approach, allowing new business to track them down and it has worked just fine for them as evidenced by their nationally recognized top sales status. That should encourage you!

Do not misunderstand: I am not saying that they laid in a hammock and did nothing to generate leads. Instead, I am saying that they had methods that acted like people magnets, warmly attracting potential clients to them as opposed to going on a cold hunt for clients.

1. DAVENPORT, L. D. (2017, MARCH). RESIDENTIAL REAL ESTATE SALES, LEAD GENERATION AND PERSONALITY: TRENDS FROM TOP PRODUCERS (DOCTORAL DISSERTATION, CALUNIVERSITY, 2017).

YOUR TURN

- Are you more suited for cold or warm lead generation?
- Do you have the gear to handle both or just one?

Be honest with yourself because you will only be miserable with a mismatched lead generation climate.

IT'S NOT ME...
IT'S YOU

Chapter 6

Are you spending hours on the "hamster wheel"? In other words, you are busy on the go, but you are not actually moving from point A to point B, making real lead generation progress. If so, stop asking, "**Why** can't I do this?" or "**Why** doesn't this work for me?", likely demotivating and discouraging you.

No need to sink into a depression if you are hustling every waking day to find new business. Instead, ask, "**How** can I improve my lead generation strategy? **How** can I approach this differently to win?"

Top Producer Best Practices

Getting back to our collegiate survey results from some of the top 1,000 residential real estate salespeople in the US:

> "SOME LEAD GENERATION
> ACTIVITIES WORK BETTER FOR
> SOME PERSONALITY TYPES THAN
> OTHERS; "

And,

> "SOME LEAD GENERATION ACTIVITIES
> ARE LESS FAVORED BY SOME PERSONALITY
> TYPES THAN OTHERS."[1]

All respondents surveyed have been successful with lead generation but not all surveyed used the same techniques. In other words, we cannot marry **methods**! It is not "until death do us part" with our lead generation activities, especially now, considering how technology and communication continue to evolve.

---

1. DAVENPORT, L. D. (2017, MARCH). RESIDENTIAL REAL ESTATE SALES, LEAD GENERATION AND PERSONALITY: TRENDS FROM TOP PRODUCERS (DOCTORAL DISSERTATION, CALUNIVERSITY, 2017).

MANAGERS' MOMENT

Those two statements are quite simple and seem very intuitive despite being two **Top Producer Best Practices.** However, does your organization inadvertently train everyone to be a cookie-cutter salesperson, doing only the familiar lead generation activities instead of speaking to the uniquely varied salespeople and their personalities? Often, managers search to recruit and retain a vibrant sales force and the answer lies in the two statements above.

We must help salespeople find the lead generation activities that work better and are more favorable for their personality type. This liberates us from dogmatically chasing one or two dominant lead generation methods. If you join this revolutionary thinking, personality work-fit can become your firm's competitive advantage to attracting and keeping a burgeoning sales team.

GREEN
MEANS GO

Your Inventory of Optimal Lead-Gen.

Have you ever sped through a red traffic light? If you have not, then I am sure you understand the harm you can cause to yourself, others, and even your wallet if you get a ticket. You get it — the red light stops you from a wreck. In this chapter, we will examine what may be wrecking your lead generation.

Lead generation is the backbone of your longevity in sales. Thus, it is vital that you determine sooner rather than later what works the best for you. Ideally, have at least three to five lead generation (lead-gen.) activities that you like and can master to get off the sales hamster wheel and even rollercoaster of having business today but none next week. Begin to keep your sales pipeline full and eliminate "feast or famine" fluctuations by taking a page out of the top producer playbook — have enough of the right activities to get more leads.

———

TOP PRODUCER BEST PRACTICES

Of the top 1,000 residential real estate sales-people surveyed:

> **94 PERCENT** OF THEM HAD AT LEAST *THREE* **LEAD GENERATION ACTIVITIES** THEY USED REGULARLY THROUGHOUT THE PREVIOUS YEAR TO MAINTAIN A THRIVING SALES BUSINESS;

And,

> **MORE THAN THREE-QUARTERS** (A.K.A. THE MAJORITY!) HAD *FIVE* **OR MORE LEAD GENERATION CATEGORIES IN CONSTANT USE.**[1]

In essence, putting "all your eggs in one basket," or one lead generation method, leaves you exposed (remember, Mr. Wolf!).

Take a moment to critically think about the following **Lead-Gen. Signals,** which inventories your optimal lead generation climate and method. Use your **Lead-Gen. Signals** to review your current lead generation practices and to identify what needs to be dismissed and what more can be added to get you to at least three to five methods you execute each month.

———

1. Davenport, L. D. (2017, March). Residential Real Estate Sales, Lead Generation and Personality: Trends from Top Producers (Doctoral dissertation, CalUniversity, 2017).

LEAD-GEN. SIGNALS

YOUR INVENTORY OF OPTIMAL LEAD GENERATION

The following are some of the most popular lead generation categories (segmented by cold and warm) for residential real estate sales.

COLD LEAD-GEN. METHODS:

MY NAME IS (WHAT?), MY NAME IS (WHO?)

---

1. Cold calling (e.g. FSBO, expired or withdrawn listings, call lists, etc.)
2. Marketing (farming) mailings or emails (e.g. just sold/listed postcard mailings, etc.)
3. Unscheduled marketing (farming) visits (e.g. door-knocking, visits to business offices, etc.)
4. Traditional advertisements (e.g. TV,

radio, newspaper & magazine ads, billboards, bus/car wraps, key chains, etc.)

5. Online ads and lead generation sites (e.g. Boomtown, Zillow Premier Agent, Realtor.com®, Facebook Ads, Google Adwords, etc.)

6. Internet trolling (e.g. unsolicited and typically inappropriate promotion of your services on social media sites and websites) – although some salespeople do this, I do NOT recommend this method

---

WARM LEAD-GEN. METHODS:

WHERE EVERYBODY KNOWS YOUR NAME

---

1. Personal mailings or emails (e.g. personal note, newsletters, thank you/thinking of you cards, etc.)

2. Planned personal visits (e.g. lunches, coffee meetings, drop-bys, etc.)

3. Inquiries from your online reviews
4. Your website/blog/site
5. Lawn signs
6. Open houses
7. Home buying/selling seminars or webinars
8. Social media videos
9. Social media posts
10. Blogging/article writing
11. Past client referrals
12. Sphere of influence (e.g. family, friends, neighbors, co-workers, classmates, etc) referrals
13. Agent/broker referrals (including desk/office duty)
14. Networking, club, and community events
15. Volunteering
16. Sponsorship (e.g. sports, festivals, classes, etc.)
17. Warm calling (e.g. reconnecting with sphere of influence, past clients, leads, etc.)
18. Your MLS

19. Vendor referrals (e.g. from attorneys, lenders, REO banks, etc.)

Cold lead generation tactics dominant some sales marketing plans and models, intimidating introverts but, interestingly, warm methods are typically more plenteous. How comforting! Are there other lead-gen. categories you want to add? Keep in mind that as technological advances continue in how we communicate, these categories will naturally expand so please be sure to stay current and update these lists.

Your Turn

Now, let us review your **Lead-Gen. Signals.** Reflect on each category and ask yourself, "In which categories am I most comfortable and make the most meaningful connections?"

Red Light

- Which of this lead-gen. categories and activities have you tried but do not like?
- How can you eliminate off "your plate" any activities you have tried but do not like?

- Can any of these be outsourced to still get the value but not tax you?

Yellow Light

- What lead-gen. categories and activities have you tried but have not had enough time to determine their effectiveness?
- How can you spend some time with the lead generation activities that you have tried but do not know the full results?
- What lead-gen. activities have you not tried but you want to try?
- How can you schedule the time to try new activities that interest you?
- What lead-gen. activities have you not tried and you do not want to try? Why? Do you need to re-examine trying these activities? Do you need to outsource these activities?

Green Light

- What lead-gen. categories and activities have you tried and liked?
- How can you allot more time for the activities you have tried and liked? **Hint:** This is where you should spend the bulk of your lead generation time!
- What three to five preferred lead generation activities will you implement in your business this year?

What date will you annually review your **Lead-Gen. Signals** to ensure your lead generation is the most effective for you and the current times? **Hint:** Do not wait for someone to do an annual review with you! Plan time each year to review your lead generation to see what you need to continue, nix, or revamp to keep your sales pipeline full.

TYING IT ALL TOGETHER

Let's put a "bow" around our discussion to help you walk away with an actionable game plan to succeed.

A BOOST
BETTER THAN
COFFEE

Chapter 7

Have you ever been to an event, like a wedding, that was buffet style? Typically, with a food buffet (at least at a good one), there are many delectable options. There are enough options that you can pick-and-choose and prioritize what you will eat first and maybe come back for seconds.

Now, compare that to a wedding banquet where it is a solitary plated meal that you do not have the power of choice. To make matters worse, it took you several hours to get to the quaint wedding venue out in no-man's land with no home, business, or even a McDonald's in sight; and, you are famished. As a result, even though you were not in the mood for spice-less chicken and flavorless green beans today, that is your only choice. You pick at it and try to "doctor it up" as you resign to eating it. A buffet verses a single plated meal reflect choices, or lack thereof.

Likewise, in our residential real estate sales businesses, if we do not have enough lead choices, we pick at what is available and try (*oh, how we try!*) to make it work. However, the real estate sales game is still a **numbers game**. Thus, instead of trying to work with looky-loos or disloyal prospects, we can minimize, and perhaps end, our frustration by doing more of the activities that help us generate more leads and prospective new business. Often our business ills are solved with more quality leads, provided we are already superstars at lead conversion and transaction management (neither are the topic of this book but will likely follow in this book series).

Have you hit a dry spell in your business? This is often because we are not doing enough to find new business. Now that you have the "green light" and know your preferred three to five lead generation activities from the last chapter, the next step is **consistent** action! This is not a book on planning, scheduling, or time management (check out my book, Plan to Win! for those types of tips). But I would be remiss if I ignored a popular way for my coaching clients to restore their zeal and focus in scouting out new business.

Try the 1-2-3 **Slam** for a quick business pick-me-up that works better than coffee:

First, pick one of your Green Light lead-gen. activities from earlier that will connect you with NEW people (social media posts, live video, networking event, buying/selling seminar, and whatever else USUALLY gets you business).

Next, do that thing! Then keep doing that Green Light lead-gen. activity until you walk away with at least two new leads (a.k.a. actual contact information). This could take you five minutes or 50 minutes. It is not about the time but the **results**: Get two new leads!

Then, reconnect with three leads/contacts that you have not connected with in a while. You could call, message on social media, email, or send smoke signals, ha! The key is to reconnect.

If your leads pipeline looks empty or you feel overwhelmed and floundering, then the 1-2-3 **Slam** is a quick way to jumpstart your pipeline for the day.

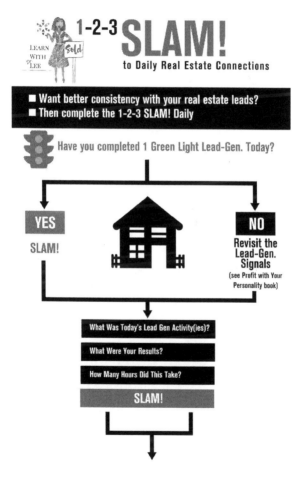

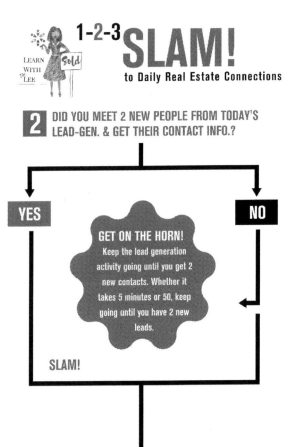

1-2-3 SLAM!
to Daily Real Estate Connections

LEARN WITH Dr. LEE

Sold

2 DID YOU MEET 2 NEW PEOPLE FROM TODAY'S LEAD-GEN. & GET THEIR CONTACT INFO.?

YES

NO

GET ON THE HORN!
Keep the lead generation activity going until you get 2 new contacts. Whether it takes 5 minutes or 50, keep going until you have 2 new leads.

SLAM!

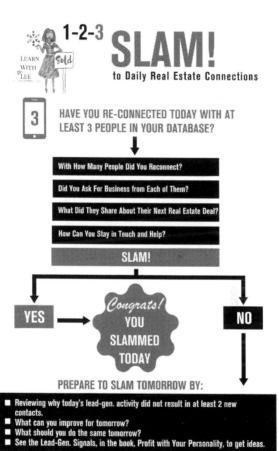

YOUR TURN

- What three to five lead generation activities do you do weekly to grow your new leads?
- How many leads typically result from these activities on a weekly basis?
- If you are not satisfied with your weekly new leads count, revisit the **Lead-Gen. Signals** chart and see if there are any Green Lights you missed, Yellow Lights you should consider, and Red Lights you could outsource. What additional activities can you add, tweak, or outsource?

- Try the 1-2-3 Slam at least one time this week. What were your results? What did you learn?

TO BE CONTINUED...

MORE BY LEE

PLAN TO WIN!

Transform Your Real Estate Sales Game
Plan TODAY

WHAT OTHER'S ARE SAYING

5-STARS!

"There's a lot of great information in this book. If you actually do what Lee is suggesting, interact with the book, I find it hard to believe sales wouldn't follow. Additionally, this is a relatively novel approach for real estate sales books; interactivity. I like it, and I think the author did a stellar job collecting and distilling a lot of great information!"

~Amazon Book Purchaser

"I purchased your book and have all the answers I need! Thank you!!!" ~ S. Dixon, Maryland Real Estate Salesperson

This well-crafted workbook is a top-notch catalyst and guide to developing essential sales skills necessary for sales agents to thrive in today's real estate market. Jumpstart or revamp your:

- Competitive advantage to stand out among a crowd of agents,
- Understanding of your strengths and weaknesses,
- Know-how to generate and convert leads into closing clients,
- Listing acquisitions,
- Negotiation prowess,
- Social media impact,
- Connection with home buyers,
- And much more!

Be unstoppable! Grab your copy of Dr. Lee Davenport's **Plan to Win!** from Amazon.com today.

*

COACHING & WORKSHOPS

"Thank you Lee Davenport for one of the best
social media classes ever!!!"
~Sharon Henry, EMPIRE Board of REALTISTS
2017 President

"Very informative! Lee gives ideas I never thought
of!"
~Patricia, Georgia Real Estate Salesperson

"You dropped some knowledge bombs, Lee! Thank
you!"
~Marcus, Texas Real Estate Salesperson

"Most educational class in a long time!"
~Colleen, RE/MAX Agent

"I tried Buffini but your coaching style is a better fit for me!"

~G. Monardo, Nevada Real Estate Salesperson

"I actually learned something in this class! So often I take classes just to get the CE credits but I am telling everyone yours in the one to be in if you are serious about marketing your business"

-K. Mitchell, Better Homes & Gardens Real Estate Agent

Here are some of Dr. Lee's most popular workshops that you can schedule for your team, firm, or association by emailing info@LearnWithLee.REALTOR:

1. Automation that Generates Leads in Your Sleep

Discover apps that work to grow your business while you sleep.

2. Facebook Ads Intensive

Facebook ads are cheap, making them the best thing since "sliced bread" to reach a large audience inexpensively. Well, that's if you actually are generating leads. Understand why your past Facebook ads have not generated leads and create a robust lead-generating ad on the spot.

3. Killer Content

People are tired of giving away their contact information without being offered value. Learn how to create content that people won't want to pass up.

4. Do You!

Use your personality and develop your unique selling proposition to grow your business and generate leads.

5. Creating a Show-Stopper Facebook Business Page

How do you use Facebook to attract people

you have never met before? It all starts with a Facebook Business Page, which you create during this class.

6. How to Grow Your Business with Instagram
This workshop gives live feedback on your Instagram site to help you improve your reach.

7. Getting Started on Instagram
This workshop will help you create an Instagram account and publish your first post. *Pre-requisite: Participants must bring a smartphone.

8. Listing Leader (Georgia 3-Hour CE coming soon)
Want to learn the right way to become a Listing Agent. This national workshop focuses on the 7 key areas.

9. Buyers are Liars?! (Georgia 3-Hour CE available)
Working successfully with buyers so that

you don't have headaches is a skill that this class covers.

10. Real Social: From Likes to Leads (Georgia 3-Hour CE available)

Explore low-cost and free techniques to generate more leads from today's most effective social media sites for business.

Made in the USA
San Bernardino, CA
10 August 2017